Date: 10/28/20

BR 510 HUN
Hunt, Santana,
Making soups with math! /

COOKING WITH MATH!

MAKING SOUPS WITH MATH!

By Santana Hunt

Gareth Stevens
PUBLISHING

[leveled reader math]

Please visit our website, www.garethstevens.com. For a free color catalog of all our high-quality books, call toll free 1-800-542-2595 or fax 1-877-542-2596.

Library of Congress Cataloging-in-Publication Data

Names: Hunt, Santana.
Title: Making soups with math! / Santana Hunt.
Description: New York : Gareth Stevens Publishing, 2020. | Series: Cooking with math! | Includes glossary and index.
Identifiers: ISBN 9781538245668 (pbk.) | ISBN 9781538245682 (library bound) | ISBN 9781538245675 (6 pack)
Subjects: LCSH: Cooking–Mathematics–Juvenile literaure. | Mathematics–Juvenile literature. | Cooking–Juvenile literature. | Soups–Juvenile literature.
Classification: LCC TX652.5 H86 2020 | DDC 510–dc23

Published in 2020 by
Gareth Stevens Publishing
111 East 14th Street, Suite 349
New York, NY 10003

Designer: Katelyn E. Reynolds
Editor: Kate Mikoley

Photo credits: Cover, p. 1 Francesco83/Shutterstock.com; pp. 1–24 (gingham background) Mika Besfamilnaya/Shutterstock.com; pp. 1–24 (recipe background) A. Zhuravleva/Shutterstock.com; p. 5 Iakov Filimonov/Shutterstock.com; p. 7 Joshua Resnick/Shutterstock.com; p. 8 Duplass/Shutterstock.com; p. 11 Daria Mladenovic/ Shutterstock.com; p. 12 RTimages /Shutterstock.com; p. 15 Charles Brutlag/ Shutterstock.com; p. 19 CCat82/Shutterstock.com; p. 21 (salsa) V_S/Shutterstock.com.

Printed in the United States of America

CPSIA compliance information: Batch #CW20GS: For further information contact Gareth Stevens, New York, New York at 1-800-542-2595.

CONTENTS

Boldface words appear in the glossary.

Super Soup!

Soup is an excellent food to help you warm up. Some soups can even help you stay cool! You need math to make soup. Measuring, telling time, multiplication, and subtraction are just a few of the skills you might use!

Ask an adult before using the stove!

5

Chicken Noodle Soup

When it comes to favorite soups, chicken noodle is a common winner. A **recipe** will help you make something yummy! Recipes tell you how much of each **ingredient** you need. This may be given in cups, tablespoons, or other measurements.

You have a measuring cup that measures 2 cups. You also have a measuring spoon that measures 1 tablespoon. Which should you use to measure the chicken **broth**? How many times will you fill it? Check your answers on page 22!

CHICKEN NOODLE SOUP

(makes about 4–6 servings)

Ingredients:

2 carrots, chopped
2 cups cooked chicken **cubes**
2 cups uncooked noodles
6 cups chicken broth

Instructions:

1. Put broth, noodles, chicken, and carrots in a pot. Heat on the stove until **boiling**.

2. Lower heat and cover the pot. Leave on low heat for about 10 minutes. Stir every few minutes.

3. Once the noodles and carrots are a little soft, remove from heat. If you want, you can add some salt and pepper.

Great Gazpacho

Did you know not all soups are hot? Gazpacho is a kind of soup that's served cold and often includes lots of vegetables. You'll need a blender or food processor for this recipe. A food processor is a kitchen tool used for cutting and mixing foods.

11

You need to let your gazpacho cool in the refrigerator for at least 30 minutes. If you put it in the refrigerator at 2:20 p.m., what time will you be able to take it out? Use the clock to help you.

GREAT GAZPACHO

(makes 8 small servings)

Ingredients:

4 tomatoes
1 clove garlic
1 cucumber
1/2 onion
1/2 bell pepper
2 tablespoons **balsamic vinegar**
1 tablespoon olive oil

Instructions:

1. Ask an adult to chop the tomatoes, garlic, cucumber, onion, and bell pepper.

2. With an adult's help, put all ingredients in a blender or food processor.

3. Mix in the blender or food processor until smooth. It's OK to have some small chunks left.

4. Refrigerate for 30 minutes.

13

Cheesy Broccoli Soup

Recipes often tell you how many servings you'll have when you're done. However, you may want to make more. You can use multiplication to make double, or two times, the amount. Just multiply the amount of each ingredient by 2!

This recipe makes 8 servings. You're having a party and want to make enough for 16 servings. You have to double the recipe! How many cups of broccoli do you need now?

$$\begin{array}{r} 4 \text{ cups broccoli} \\ \times\ 2 \\ \hline ? \text{ cups broccoli} \end{array}$$

CHEESY BROCCOLI SOUP

(makes about 8 servings)

Ingredients:

4 cups broccoli, cut into small pieces
3 1/2 cups vegetable broth
1 cup heavy cream
3 cups cheddar cheese, shredded

Instructions:

1. Put broth, cream, and broccoli in a pot. Heat until **simmering**.

2. Lower heat and let simmer for about 15 minutes.

3. Spoon a bit of cheese into the pot and mix until it's melted. Keep doing this until you've used all the cheese.

4. Remove from heat.

Tasty Taco Soup

Recipes are great guides that make cooking easier. You don't have to follow them exactly though! You can add different ingredients, or take out ones you don't like. You can also add toppings to change up the taste!

19

Some cheese would make a great topping for this soup! You had 4 cups of cheese. You used 3 of those cups making the cheesy broccoli soup. How much cheese do you have left?

$$\begin{array}{r} 4 \text{ cups} \\ - 3 \text{ cups} \\ \hline ? \text{ cups} \end{array}$$

TASTY TACO SOUP

(makes about 4 servings)

Ingredients:

3 cups chicken broth
1 cup black beans
1 cup salsa
1 cup cooked chicken, shredded

Instructions:

1. Mix together all ingredients in a pot.

2. Put on the stove over medium heat for 5 to 10 minutes, stirring a few times.

3. Remove from heat.

salsa

Glossary

balsamic vinegar: an Italian vinegar, or sour liquid, that also tastes fairly sweet

boil: to be heated so that bubbles form and rise to the top of a liquid

broth: a liquid, commonly used in soups, in which food has been cooked

cube: a shape with six square sides

ingredient: a food that is mixed with other foods

recipe: an explanation of how to make food

simmer: to cook something until almost boiling for a time. Also, the state of coming close to boiling.

Answer Key

p. 8 The measuring cup. You will fill it three times.

p. 12 2:50 p.m.

p. 16 8 cups of broccoli

p. 20 1 cup of cheese

For More Information

Books

Borgert-Spaniol, Megan. *Math You Can Munch.* Minneapolis, MN: Super Sandcastle, 2019.

Owen, Ruth. *Kids Cook!* New York, NY: Windmill Books, 2017.

Websites

2nd Grade Math
www.mathplayground.com/grade_2_games.html
Find math games here!

Recipes & Cooking for Kids
kidshealth.org/en/kids/recipes/
Discover more recipes you can make on this website.

Index